ANITA DROBECK & NICO RADEMACHER

VIETNAM PANORAMA

Text by Iris Lemanczyk

EDITION**PANORAMA**

VIETNAM

Ein Bambusstab, an dessen Enden zwei Reiskörbe hängen, so sieht Vietnams Umriss auf der Landkarte aus. Im Norden das fruchtbare Flussdelta des Roten Flusses als ein Reiskorb, der andere das Mekongdelta im Süden. Dazwischen ein schmaler, langer, eher karger Landstrich von mehr als 900 Kilometer Länge, der an manchen Stellen nur 50 Kilometer breit ist. Wilde, zerklüftete Gebirgslandschaften, in denen Bergvölker zurückgezogen leben, traumhafte, endlose Sandstrände, einsame Buchten, Pagoden, Tempel, schwimmende Dörfer, sattgrüne Reisfelder, Kanäle, Flüsse, Palmenhaine, tausendjährige Traditionen im Kontrast zu fieberhaftem Aufbruch. Das alles ist Vietnam. Und der Eindruck, vor allem in den Städten, dass dieses Land nie schläft.

Zu Tausenden fluten Mopeds durch die Straßen von Hanoi und Ho Chi Minh-Stadt, dem früheren Saigon. Rund um die Uhr. Unermüdliche Händler, emsige Garküchenbetreiber und Handwerker kennen keine Öffnungszeiten. Sie scheinen Lust am Tempo zu haben. Ein Volk will voran kommen. Hanoi besteht aus zwei, vielleicht drei Millionen Kleinstunternehmern: Moped-Rangiererinnen, die Zweiräder auf den Gehwegen verstauen, Männer, die Glücksmünzen oder Lose verkaufen, andere klauben Plastikmüll zusammen oder warten mit ihrer Luftpumpe auf Kundschaft. Inmitten der Stadt liegt der Hoan-Kiem-See. Im Morgengrauen verrichten ältere Frauen und Männer schweigend ihre Tai-Chi Übungen. Ausnahmsweise ist es

VIETNAM

Vietnam's outline on the map looks like a bamboo pole, with a rice basket hanging from each end. In the North, the fertile Red River delta making up one of the baskets, balanced on the other end by the Mekong delta in the South. Between them lies a long, narrow and rather barren strip of land almost 600 miles in length, which at some points is only 30 miles wide. Wild, jagged mountain landscapes, in which mountain peoples live a withdrawn way of life, beautiful endless sandy beaches, lonely bays, pagodas, temples, floating villages, verdant green rice paddies, canals, rivers, palm groves, thousands of years of tradition contrasting with the frantic pace of development. All this is Vietnam – and the impression, particularly in the cities, that this country never sleeps.

Mopeds in their thousands flow through the streets of Hanoi and Ho Chi Minh City, the former Saigon. All around the clock. Tireless dealers, busy food-stall operators and artisans know no fixed opening times. They seem to take pleasure in the tempo. A people who want to get ahead. Hanoi is home to two, perhaps three million small businesses: Moped-parkers who park and manoeuvre the vehicles on the pavements, men selling lucky coins or lottery tickets, others who collect plastic waste or wait for customers with their foot pumps ready to hand. In the middle of the city lies the Hoan-Kiem Lake, where older men and women silently perform their Tai-Chi exercises at dawn. It is unusually quiet. Memories of times long past

VIETNAM

Le Vietnam ressemble sur les cartes géographiques à un balancier en bambou avec deux paniers de riz accrochés aux extrémités : au nord, le delta fertile du fleuve Rouge et au sud, le delta du Mékong. Entre les deux, une étroite bande de terre, longue et plutôt aride, de plus de 900 km de long et de 50 km de large seulement en certains endroits. Le Vietnam réunit toutes sortes de paysages : des montagnes sauvages et déchiquetées dans lesquelles des peuplades montagnardes mènent une vie retirée, d'interminables et magnifiques plages de sable, des baies solitaires, des pagodes, des temples, des villages flottants, des rizières d'un vert éclatant, des canaux, des rivières, des palmeraies, des traditions millénaires contrastant avec le vent du renouveau qui souffle sur le pays. Le Vietnam c'est tout cela à la fois avec en plus, surtout dans les villes, l'impression que ce pays ne dort jamais.
Les cyclomoteurs envahissent par milliers les rues de Hanoi et de Ho Chi Minh-Ville, ancienne Saigon. Vingt-quatre heures sur vingt-quatre. Les rues sont également encombrées par des commerçants infatigables, des cuisiniers ambulants zélés et toutes sortes d'artisans qui ne ferment jamais boutique. Ils ont l'air apparemment de trouver à leur goût cette manière de vivre à cent à l'heure. C'est un peuple qui veut aller de l'avant. On recense à Hanoi deux, peut-être trois millions de petits métiers : des gareuses de cyclomoteurs qui se chargent de garer les deux-roues sur les chemins de passage, des vendeurs de pièces porte-bon-

VIETNAM

El contorno de Vietnam en el mapa recuerda una caña de bambú de cuyos extremos cuelgan dos cestos de arroz. El primero de los cestos de arroz sería el norte, dominado por el delta del Río Rojo, el segundo lo formaría el sur del país, básicamente ocupado por el delta del Mekong. Y entremedio de los dos cestos se encuentra una estrecha y larga lengua de tierra más bien árida de 900 kilómetros de longitud y que en algunos trechos apenas llega a los 50 kilómetros de anchura. Vietnam reúne todas las vistas: sierras salvajes y escarpadas en las que todavía viven recogidos pueblos de montaña, interminables playas de ensueño, solitarias bahías, pagodas, templos, pueblos flotantes, campos de arroz de un color verde profundo, canales, ríos, bosques de palmeras y tradiciones milenarias en fuerte contraste con el enfebrecido auge económico que actualmente experimenta el país. Todo eso es Vietnam. Y además de todo eso la impresión, sobre todo en las ciudades, de que este país nunca duerme.
Miles de ciclomotores invaden las calles de Hanoi y la ciudad de Ho Chi Minh, la antigua Saigon. Y eso las veinticuatro horas del día. Las calles están repletas de incansables buhoneros, ajetreados quiosqueros de comida tradicional así como todo tipo de artesanos que no conocen pausa: todos ellos parecen encontrarse a gusto en esta vida que discurre a toda velocidad. Éste es un pueblo que quiere progresar. Se podría decir que Hanoi no tiene habitantes, sino dos o quizás tres millones de trabajadores autónomos

VIETNAM

Una canna di bambù alle cui estremità sono appesi due cesti pieni di riso, ecco come appare il profilo del Vietnam sulla cartina geografica. Al nord il fertile delta del Fiume Rosso come cesto di riso, al sud il suo pendant rappresentato dal delta del Mekong. Tra di essi la sottile, lunga e piuttosto brulla striscia di terra lunga oltre 900 chilometri, la quale in alcuni punti è larga solamente 50 chilometri. Selvatici paesaggi montani frastagliati da innumerevoli gole nei quali le popolazioni vivono ritirate, magnifiche ed infinite spiagge di sabbia, baie solitarie, pagode, templi, paesi sospesi sull'acqua, risaie dal colore verde vivo, canali, fiumi, palmeti, tradizioni vecchie di millenni in contrasto con il febbricitante progresso. Tutto questo è il Vietman. E l'impressione, che si ha soprattutto nelle città, che questo paese non dorma mai.
A migliaia le motociclette invadono le strade di Hanoi e Ho Chi Minh, l'ex-Saigon. 24 ore su 24. Gli instancabili commercianti e i gestori di trattorie ed artigiani ligi al dovere, non conoscono orari di apertura. Sembra che la frenesia procuri loro piacere. Un popolo che vuole avanzare. Hanoi consiste in due o forse tre milioni di piccolissimi imprenditori: aggiustatori di motociclette che intasano le vie pedonali con le loro due ruote, uomini che vendono monete portafortuna o biglietti della lotteria; altri raccolgono i rifiuti di plastica o attendono i clienti con la loro pompa per gomme. Al centro della città si trova il lago Hoan Kiem. All'alba uomini e donne anziani svolgono in

still. Erinnerungen an längst vergangene Zeiten steigen auf. Erinnerungen an den Helden Le Loi, dem es 1428 gelang, die Chinesen aus dem Land zu vertreiben. Das Schwert dafür, so erzählt man sich, erhielt er von der göttlichen Schildkröte aus den Tiefen des Sees.

Später kommen die Franzosen und erklären Hanoi zur Hauptstadt. Hier, an der „Schleife des Roten Flusses" – nichts anderes bedeutet Hanoi – sitzt die Macht. Die Kolonialherren legen Boulevards und Alleen an, bauen die Kanalisation und eine Oper, machen aber einen Bogen um die Altstadt mit ihren 36 winzigen Gassen. Dieses Häuserlabyrinth ist vor mehr als tausend Jahren entstanden, um den Hofstaat zu versorgen. Auch heute noch ist es ruhelos, geschäftig, wie eh und je. Hanoi ist die Stadt des Kleinhandels und Handwerks, Ho Chi Minh ist die Stadt der Industrie. Hanoi eine alte, ehrwürdige Dame mit 2000 Jahren Geschichte. Das frühere Saigon dagegen 300 Jahre jung, die frivole Nichte Hanois, frühreif und flippig. Und geschäftstüchtig. Ihr Wirtschaftswachstum übertrifft das nationale um ein Drittel. Schnell reagierte die Stadt 1986, als das kommunistische Politbüro Doi Moi – die Erneuerung des Denkens – beschloss. Dadurch begann der Übergang von der Plan- zur Marktwirtschaft.

Hektische, schnelllebige Zeiten brechen für die geschäftige Nichte Saigon an. Kurz noch eine Nudelsuppe löffeln, dann zum Hauptpostamt. Ein Relikt französischer Kolonialzeit. In der Mitte des Gebäudes unter dem eisernen Dachstuhl und den wirbelnden Ventilatoren stehen lange Bänke. Hier arbeiten die öffentlichen Schreiber, die für Väter oder Verliebte Briefe aufsetzen. Nach Übersee, wo die Schwieger-

come to mind. Memories of the hero Le Loi, who succeeded in driving the Chinese out of the country in 1428. He obtained his sword, so legend has it, from the Turtle God out of the depths of the sea.

Later the French arrived and declared Hanoi as the capital city. Here at the "loop of the Red River" – the actual meaning of the word Hanoi – was the seat of power. The colonial rulers laid out boulevards and avenues, built the drainage system and an opera house, although made a detour around the old town with its 36 tiny streets. This labyrinth of houses grew up over 1,000 years ago, in order to serve the royal household. It is still just as restless and busy today as it always has been. Hanoi is the city of small tradesmen and artisans, while Ho Chi Minh City is the city of industry. Hanoi is the venerable old lady with 2,000 years of history. The former Saigon on the other hand is only 300 years old, the frivolous niece of Hanoi, precocious and flirtatious. And enterprising. Its economic growth exceeds the national average by one third. The city reacted quickly in 1986, when the Communist Politburo adopted the policy of "Doi Moi" – the revival of thinking, heralding the transition from a planned economy to a market economy.

Hectic, fast-moving times arrived for the bustling Saigon. Quickly bolt down a noodle soup and then off to the main Post Office. A relic of the French colonial era. In the middle of the building under the iron roof and the whirling fans stand long benches. Here the public scribes work, drafting letters for fathers or lovers. To overseas, where a daughter-in-law might be studying or a loved-one looking

heur ou de billets de loterie, des éboueurs indépendants qui ramassent les déchets plastiques ou d'autres encore qui attendent la clientèle avec leur pompe à air. En plein cœur de la ville, on trouve le lac de Hoan-Kiem. Au point du jour dans un silence respectueux, des anciens, hommes et femmes, font leurs exercices de Tai-Chi. Tout est calme à cet instant précis, exceptionnellement, et des souvenirs d'une époque depuis longtemps révolue remontent à la surface. Le souvenir par exemple du héros Le Loi qui, en 1428, parvient à chasser les Chinois du pays. On raconte qu'il se serait servi pour ce faire d'une épée qui lui aurait été donnée par la tortue sacrée des Dieux qui vit dans les profondeurs du lac.

Ils sont remplacés plus tard par les Français qui déclarent Hanoi capitale du pays. C'est ici, en bordure du « méandre du fleuve Rouge » – Hanoi signifie en effet « cité à l'intérieur du fleuve » –, que réside désormais le pouvoir. La nouvelle puissance coloniale aménage des boulevards et des allées, construit des canalisations et un opéra, mais ne se hasarde pas dans la vieille ville et ses 36 ruelles minuscules. Ce labyrinthe de maisons construit il y a plus de mille ans afin de pourvoir aux besoins de la cour est, aujourd'hui encore, un quartier déployant une activité aussi dynamique et affairée qu'autrefois. Hanoi est la ville du petit commerce et de l'artisanat, Ho Chi Minh celle de l'industrie. Hanoi est une dame vénérable vieille de 2 000 ans tandis que l'ancienne Saigon n'a que 300 ans. On dit d'elle d'ailleurs qu'elle est la nièce frivole de Hanoi : un peu précoce et branchée, mais douée pour les affaires. Elle a su réagir rapidement en 1986 lorsque le Politbureau communiste

y pequeños empresarios: aparcadoras de ciclomotores que se encargan de estacionar –casi se podría decir acumular– las motos en las aceras, vendedores de monedas de la fortuna o billetes de lotería, basureros por cuenta propia que recogen plástico o gente dispuesta a ayudar por unas monedas con su bomba de aire a los motociclistas. En el centro de la ciudad se encuentra el lago Hoan-Kiem. Allí, rodeados de un aura de respetuoso silencio, ancianos de ambos sexos practican sus ejercicios de Tai-Chi. Se podría decir que este sosiego es en esta urbe una excepción que despierta la memoria de épocas que ya pasaron hace mucho tiempo. Por ejemplo el recuerdo del héroe Le Loi que en 1428 logró expulsar a los chinos. La leyenda cuenta que este paladín recibió su espada de la tortuga sagrada de los dioses que vive en el fondo del lago.

Más tarde llegaron los franceses y declararon capital a Hanoi. Aquí, en el "meandro del Río Rojo" –pues ese es el significado de Hanoi– reside el poder. La potencia colonial construyó paseos y avenidas, la canalización y una ópera, pero no se metió en el centro histórico con sus 36 estrechísimas callejuelas. Los orígenes de este laberinto de casas, que fue edificado para asegurar el abastecimiento de la corte, se remontan a hace más de mil años. Aún hoy la vida sigue desarrollándose aquí al mismo paso dinámico y atareado de siempre. Hanoi es la ciudad del comercio en detalle y de los pequeños empresarios, Ho Chi Minh sin embargo es la ciudad de la industria. Hanoi es una dama añeja y elegante con 2000 años de historia. Por el contrario la antigua Saigon es una mocita de apenas 300 años. Por así decirlo, la frívola sobrina de Hanoi: un poco precoz y

silenzio le loro esercitazioni di tai-chi. In queste ore regna eccezionalmente la calma. Ed emergono ricordi di tempi lontanissimi. Ricordi dell'eroe Le Loi, che nel 1428 riuscì a cacciare i cinesi dal paese. La spada che aveva utilizzato a questo scopo, si racconta, l'aveva ricevuta dalla tartaruga divina dagli abissi del lago.

Poi arrivano i francesi e dichiarano Hanoi capitale. Qui, sulla "sponda del Fiume Rosso" – è semplicemente questo che significa "Hanoi" – risiede il potere. I governatori coloniali costruiscono corsi e viali, installano la canalizzazione e un teatro dell'opera, evitano però di toccare il centro storico con i suoi 36 piccolissimi vicoli. Questo labirinto di case si era costituito più di mille anni fa allo scopo di approvvigionare la corte. Ancora oggi il quartiere non conosce pause, è attivo come non mai. Hanoi è un'anziana ed onorevole dama con 2000 anni di storia. L'ex-Saigon, la frivola "nipotina" di Hanoi, ha solo 300 anni, è maturata precocemente, è pimpante. E una città d'affari. La sua crescita economica supera quella nazionale di un terzo. Rapida è stata la reazione della città nel 1986, quando il politbüro comunista decise il Doi Moi – che significa il rinnovo del pensiero –. Ciò segnò l'inizio del passaggio dall'economia pianificata all'economia di mercato.

Per Saigon sta cominciando un'era frenetica e dominata da un'estrema velocità. Ancora velocemente un ultimo sorso di minestra e poi subito alla posta. Un relitto dell'era coloniale francese. Al centro dell'edificio, sotto l'armatura di ferro del tetto e i ventilatori che girano come mulinelli, vi sono lunghe panche. Qui lavorano gli scrittori pubblici, che redigono lettere per i padri o gli innamorati. Destina-

tochter studiert oder der Geliebte Arbeit sucht. Briefe auf vietnamesisch, englisch oder französisch, ganz wie es der Kundschaft beliebt.

Seit 1975 nennen die Kommunisten die Metropole im Süden Ho Chi Minh-Stadt, trotzdem hält sich der alte Name, Saigon, hartnäckig. Das heißt aber nicht, dass hier Onkel Ho, der Unabhängigkeitskämpfer und Nationalheld, nicht genauso verehrt wird, wie im restlichen Vietnam, also von fast allen 85 Millionen Vietnamesen. Ho Chi Minh führt im Laufe seines Lebens etwa 50 verschiedene Namen, meist Tarnnamen. Geboren wird er 1890 als Nguyen Sinh Cung. Nach dem Abitur verlässt er sein Land, weil er die französischen Kolonialherren und ihre lokalen Helfer ablehnt. Er arbeitet in Amerika und Europa als Schiffsjunge, Konditor, Fotograf und Journalist und interessiert sich zunehmend für die Politik. In Paris ist er Gründungsmitglied der Kommunistischen Partei Frankreichs, seine Karriere als Revolutionär beginnt. 1930 gründet Ho die Kommunistische Partei Indochinas. Nach 30 Jahren im Ausland, betritt er 1941 seine Heimat wieder und nennt sich Ho Chi Minh, der nach Erleuchtung Strebende. Sein zäher Partisanenkampf und der seiner Anhänger richten sich gegen den Kolonialismus. 1954 gelingt ihm der Sieg über die Franzosen, Onkel Ho, der Mann mit dem Ziegenbärtchen, wird Präsident der Demokratischen Republik Vietnam. Er stirbt 1969 und liegt einbalsamiert im Mausoleum in Hanoi. Sicherlich wäre ihm, der selbstgefertigte Sandalen aus alten Autoreifen trug, dieser Prunk und Trubel um seine Person suspekt. Bis vor kurzem wurde der Leichnam einmal im Jahr nach Moskau verschickt,

for work. Letters in Vietnamese, English or French, whichever the customer prefers.

In 1975, the Communists renamed this metropolis in the South Ho Chi Minh City, although the old name of Saigon persists stubbornly. This does not mean however that Uncle Ho, the independence fighter and national hero, is not honoured just as much here as in the rest of Vietnam, and therefore by almost all 85 million Vietnamese. Ho Chi Minh used about 50 different names in the course of his lifetime, mostly aliases. He was born in 1890 as Nguyen Sinh Cung. After obtaining his school-leaving certificate, he left his country, rejecting the French colonial rulers and their local helpers. He worked in America and Europe as a cabin boy, pastry cook, photographer and journalist, becoming increasingly interested in politics. In Paris, he became a founder member of the French Communist Party, launching his career as a revolutionary. In 1930, Ho founded the Communist Party of Indochina. After 30 years abroad, he again set foot in his home country in 1941, and took the name of Ho Chi Minh – "he who strives for enlightenment". The stubborn partisan struggle of Ho and his followers was directed against colonialism. Victory over the French finally came in 1954, and Uncle Ho, the man with the goatee beard, became President of the Democratic Republic of Vietnam. He died in 1969, and now lies embalmed in the mausoleum in Hanoi. He would certainly be suspicious about all this pomp and ceremony about his person, he who wore home-made sandals made out of old vehicle tyres. Until recently, his body was sent once every year to Moscow, in order to be re-embalmed.

amorce le passage d'une économie dirigée à une économie de marché grâce à la proclamation du «Doi Moi» – réforme de l'économie et de la société –. Il n'est donc pas surprenant que sa croissance économique actuelle soit d'un tiers supérieure à la croissance nationale.
La nièce diligente de Saigon entre alors dans une ère agitée et effrénée. De nombreux Vietnamiens trouvent à peine le temps de manger en vitesse un potage aux vermicelles avant de filer à la poste principale, vestige de l'ère coloniale française. Au milieu du bâtiment sous la charpente en fer du toit et les ventilateurs qui tournent, des écrivains publics travaillent sur de longs bancs. Ils écrivent des missives pour les pères ou les amoureux. Des messages vers l'outre-mer où la belle-fille fait des études, où le promis cherche du travail. Des lettres en vietnamien, en anglais ou en français, les désirs des clients sont des ordres.
En 1975, les communistes décident que la métropole dans le sud s'appellera désormais officiellement Ho Chi Minh-Ville, mais beaucoup continuent à l'appeler par son ancien nom, Saigon. Cela ne signifie pas toutefois que l'oncle Ho, héros national qui a combattu pour l'indépendance de son pays, n'est pas aussi vénéré ici que dans le reste du pays. Au contraire, ils sont presque 85 millions de Vietnamiens à lui vouer un profond respect. Ho Chi Minh a porté au cours de sa vie une cinquantaine de noms différents dont la plupart étaient des pseudonymes, probablement afin de pouvoir continuer à vivre dans la clandestinité. Né en 1890 sous le nom de Nguyen Sinh Cung, il quitte sa patrie une fois bachelier car il refuse la domination des colons français et des autorités locales qui les soutiennent. Il travaille aux

alocada, pero con mucho talento para los negocios. La ciudad supo reaccionar rápidamente después de que en 1986 el politburó comunista iniciara la transición de la economía planificada a la de mercado con la proclamación de "Doi Moi", la renovación del pensamiento. Por ello no es de extrañar que actualmente su crecimiento económico supere el nacional en un tercio.
Esta claro, para Saigon, la diligente sobrina, empezó entonces una era agitada y acelerada. Muchos vietnamitas apenas pueden permitirse un respiro para tomarse una sopa de pasta antes de seguir camino hacia la oficina principal de correos, un típico edificio de la época colonial. En medio del edificio, bajo la armadura de hierro de la cubierta y los ventiladores hay dispuestos largos bancos para el público. Aquí trabajan los escribanos oficiales que redactan misivas para los padres o los enamorados. Mensajes dirigidos a ultramar: a la nuera que estudia en la lejanía o al prometido que busca trabajo en el extranjero. Epístolas en vietnamita, inglés o francés, como prefiera el cliente.
A pesar de que desde 1975 los comunistas denominan oficialmente Ciudad de Ho Chi Minh a la metrópoli del sur, su antiguo nombre, Saigon, persiste en boca del vulgo. Eso no quiere decir que aquí no se venere del mismo modo que en el resto de Vietnam al tío Ho, el héroe nacional y luchador por la independencia. Casi todos los 85 millones de vietnamitas comparten ese profundo respeto. A lo largo de su vida Ho Chi Minh usó aproximadamente 50 nombres diferentes. Por supuesto que la mayoría de ellos eran nombres falsos para mantenerse en la clandestinidad. Nació en 1890 y le pusieron de nombre Nguyen Sinh Cung. Tras ter-

zione oltremare, dove la nuora studia all'università o la fidanzata cerca lavoro. Lettere in vietnamita, inglese o francese, a seconda di cosa desiderano i clienti.
Dal 1975 i comunisti chiamano la metropoli al sud Ho Chi Minh, ciononostante il vecchio nome Saigon persiste ostinatamente. Ciò non significa però che qui lo zio Ho, il fautore dell'indipendenza ed eroe nazionale, non venga onorato allo stesso modo come nel resto del Vietnam, quindi da quasi tutti gli 85 milioni di vietnamiti. Ho Chi Minh ha avuto nel corso della sua vita circa 50 nomi diversi, per la maggior parte mimetici. Egli nacque nel 1890 come Nguyen Sinh Cung. Dopo la maturità abbandonò il paese perché rifiutava il dominio dei colonizzatori e dei loro collaboratori locali. Lavorò in America e in Europa come marinaio, pasticcere, fotografo e giornalista interessandosi sempre più di politica. A Parigi fu uno dei fondatori del partito comunista francese, e a questo punto ebbe inizio la sua carriera di rivoluzionario. Nel 1930 Ho fondò il partito comunista indocinese. Dopo 30 anni trascorsi all'estero, nel 1941 egli ritornò nella sua patria con il nome di Ho Chi Minh, che significa colui che aspira all'illuminazione. La sua tenace lotta di partigiano condotta assieme ai suoi seguaci aveva lo scopo di combattere il colonialismo. Nel 1954 riuscì a sconfiggere i francesi, lo zio Ho, l'uomo con la barbetta da capra, diventa presidente della repubblica democratica del Vietnam. Morì nel 1969 e la sua salma imbalsamata si trova ora nel mausoleo di Hanoi. Sicuramente questa foggia attorno alla sua persona, attorno ad un uomo che portava sandali da lui stesso fabbricati da vecchi pneumatici di automobili, gli sarebbe oggi

um ihn dort frisch einzubalsamieren. Mittlerweile beherrschen die Vietnamesen die Technik selbst, sodass der Tote nicht mehr auf Reisen gehen muss.

Nach ihm benannt ist auch der Ho-Chi-Minh-Pfad, ein mehr als 15 000 Kilometer langes System aus Straßen, Wegen und Pfaden, das durch dichten Dschungel führte und während des Vietnamkrieges für Nachschub jeglicher Art sorgte. Die Amerikaner entdeckten den Pfad erst nach fünf Jahren, da seine Tarnung derart perfekt war. Da nützten auch die abgeworfenen Napalmbomben, die Entlaubungsaktionen mit dem Herbizid Agent Orange und die ständige Luftüberwachung nichts. Am Ende des Krieges hatten die Vietnamesen zwar die Amerikaner besiegt, David hat gegen Goliath gewonnen, doch zuvor warfen die Amerikaner acht Millionen Tonnen Bomben ab und hinterließen fünf Millionen Tote, darunter auch 58 000 GIs. Das Land der Bauern war verwüstet, die Häuser zerstört, die Natur vergiftet. Napalm, Agent Orange. Noch heute, drei Generationen später, kommen missgebildete Kinder zur Welt. Der amerikanische Kriegsfotograf Philip Jones Griffith sagte: „Die Franzosen haben wenigstens Kathedralen, Opernhäuser und Bahnhöfe hinterlassen. Die Amerikaner haben Vietnam zu einem Horrorladen gemacht."

Selbst durch tausend Jahre chinesische Herrschaft, später dann durch die Franzosen, Japaner, Amerikaner und die Teilung ihres Landes in Nord- und Südvietnam, ließen sich die Vietnamesen ihre Traditionen nicht nehmen. Auch nicht ihre Essgewohnheiten. Die Basis jeden Essens ist Reis, auch als Reisnudeln oder Reispapier, das zu den

Now the Vietnamese have mastered the technique themselves, so that the deceased no longer has to make the journey.

He also gave his name to the Ho-Chi-Minh Trail, an over 10,000 mile long system of roads, tracks and paths which led through the dense jungle, and was used during the Vietnam War to bring up supplies and reinforcements of all types. The Americans only discovered the trail five years later, because it was so perfectly camouflaged. Napalm bombs, the defoliation campaign using the herbicide Agent Orange and continual air reconnaissance all proved unable to close the trail. At the end of the war, victory finally went to the Vietnamese, David had won against Goliath, although not before the Americans had dropped 8 million tonnes of bombs, leaving behind them 5 million dead, including 58,000 GIs. The land of the farmers was devastated, the houses destroyed and nature poisoned. Napalm, Agent Orange. Even today, three generations later, children are still born with deformities. The American war photographer Philip Jones Griffith said: "At least the French left cathedrals, opera houses and railway stations behind them. The Americans turned Vietnam into a slaughterhouse."

Even after thousands of years of Chinese rule, later followed by the French, Japanese, Americans and the partition of their country into North and South Vietnam, the Vietnamese have not let their traditions be taken away from them. Nor their eating habits. Rice forms the basis of every dish, and is also eaten in the form of rice noodles or rice paper, which is made into the typical spring rolls. Rice is the pearl of the gods. One saying runs: "Everybody

Etats-Unis et en Europe où il exerce les métiers de mousse, pâtissier, photographe et journaliste. Parallèlement à ces activités, il manifeste un intérêt croissant pour la politique. La fondation à Paris du Parti communiste français avec d'autres camarades marque le point de départ de sa carrière révolutionnaire. En 1930, Ho crée le Parti communiste indochinois puis, après 30 ans passés à l'étranger, il rentre dans son pays natal en 1941 et prend le nom de Ho Chi Minh, littéralement « celui qui éclaire ». Avec l'aide de ses partisans, il combat avec ténacité le colonialisme. En 1954, l'oncle Ho, l'homme à la barbichette, parvient à vaincre les Français et devient le président de la République démocratique du Vietnam. Mort en 1969, son corps embaumé repose désormais dans le mausolée à Hanoi. Lui qui portait des sandales faites maison à partir de vieux pneus, trouverait probablement cette pompe et ce protocole autour de sa personne très suspects. Jusqu'à il y a peu encore, son corps était envoyé une fois par an à Moscou pour y subir des soins de conservation. Aujourd'hui, les Vietnamiens maîtrisent la technique nécessaire, ce qui les dispense de faire voyager leur héros national.

Il a également donné son nom au fameux sentier de Ho-Chi-Minh, un réseau de routes, de chemins et de pistes de plus de 15 000 kilomètres de long à travers une jungle très dense grâce auquel il a été possible de ravitailler les insurgés pendant la guerre du Vietnam. Ce sentier est si parfaitement camouflé que les Américains ne le découvrent qu'au bout de cinq ans seulement. Les bombes au napalm larguées par les avions et les hélicoptères, les défoliants et autres herbicides toxiques comme l'Agent Orange par

minar el bachillerato abandonó su patria porque rechazaba tanto a los colonizadores franceses como a sus ayudantes locales. Trabajó en América y Europa de grumete, repostero, fotógrafo y periodista mientras que crecía su interés por la política. En París fue miembro fundador del Partido Comunista de Francia. Allí comenzó su carrera revolucionaria. En 1930 Ho funda el Partido Comunista de Indochina. Tras haber pasado 30 años en el extranjero, vuelve a su país en 1941 y adopta el nombre de Ho Chi Minh: "el que aspira a la iluminación interior". A partir de entonces Ho Chi Minh y sus partidarios dirigieron su dura guerra de guerrillas contra el colonialismo. En 1954 el tío Ho, ese hombrecillo con barba de chivo, alcanza la victoria frente a los franceses y se convierte en presidente de la República Democrática de Vietnam. Murió en 1969 y actualmente sus restos mortales yacen embalsamados en el mausoleo de Hanoi. Seguramente que a él, que llevaba sandalias de fabricación casera hechas de neumáticos viejos, esa pompa y ese protocolo en torno a su persona le serían muy sospechosos. Hasta hace poco se enviaba una vez al año su cadáver a Moscú para renovar el embalsamamiento. Actualmente los mismos vietnamitas dominan la técnica de forma que el difunto ya no tiene que continuar sus viajes.

También la famosa "Ruta Ho-Chi-Minh" llevaba su nombre: un sistema de 15 000 kilómetros de carreteras, caminos y senderos a través de la más densa jungla que durante la Guerra de Vietnam sirvió para facilitar a los insurgentes abastecimiento de todo tipo. El camuflaje de la ruta era tan perfecto que los americanos tardaron cinco años en descubrirla. Pero para entonces la guerra ya había llegado a

sospetta. Fino a poco tempo fa il cadavere veniva inviato una volta all'anno a mosca per venire nuovamente imbalsamato. Adesso i vietnamiti hanno acquisito essi stessi padronanza di questa tecnica, non è quindi più necessario mandare un morto in viaggio per il mondo.

Come lui è stato chiamato anche il sentiero Ho Chi Minh, un sistema di strade, vie e sentieri lungo più di 15000 chilometri che conduce attraverso una fitta giungla e che durante la guerra in Vietnam procurava rifornimenti di ogni sorta. Gli americani scoprirono il sentiero solo dopo cinque anni, in quanto la sua mimetizzazione era perfetta. Neanche le bombe al napalm che erano state lanciate, la sfrondatura con l'erbicida Agent Orange ed il costante controllo dei cieli non servirono a nulla. Alla fine della guerra i vietnamiti avevano sì sconfitto gli americani, Davide vinse contro Golia, ma prima gli americani avevano lanciato otto milioni di tonnellate di bombe uccidendo cinque milioni di persone, tra i quali anche 58000 Gls. Il paese dei contadini era devastato, le case distrutte, la natura avvelenata. Napalm, Agent Orange. Ancora oggi, tre generazioni più tardi, nascono bambini con malformazioni. Il fotografo di guerra americano Philip Jones disse: "I francesi hanno almeno lasciato cattedrali, teatri dell'opera e stazioni ferroviarie. Gli americani hanno fatto del Vietnam una camera degli orrori."

Neanche dopo mille anni di dominio cinese, a cui seguirono i francesi, i giapponesi e gli americani, e nonostante la divisione del loro paese in Vietnam del nord e Vietnam del sud, i vietnamiti non si sono lasciati portare via le loro tradizioni. Neanche per quanto riguarda le abitudini alimentari. La base di ogni pasto è il riso, anche come pasta di riso

typischen Rollen verarbeitet wird. Reis ist die Perle der Götter. Ein Sprichwort lautet: „Jeder Mensch braucht den Reis, wie der Fisch das Wasser.“ 80 Prozent der Landbevölkerung verdienen ihren Lebensunterhalt damit. Reisfelder liegen vor allem in den Reiskörben der Flussdeltas. Die Farbe Grün bestimmt in allen Schattierungen das Landschaftsbild. Von den zarten Nuancen junger Setzlinge, über die satten und kräftigen Grüns während des Wachstums, bis zum grün-gelb bei der Ernte. Dazwischen schwerfällig stapfende Wasserbüffel mit weißen Reihern auf den Rücken. Wasserbüffel sind die Traktoren der Reisbauern, die das Schwemmland vor der Aussaat pflügen. Meistens sitzen Kinder auf den friedfertigen Rindern und lotsen sie durch die Felder.

Die spitz zulaufenden Kegelhüte aus Bast und das Aodai, das lange Gewand mit den Schlitzen, runden das klischeehafte Vietnambild ab. Doch die praktischen Hüte werden meist nur noch von der Landbevölkerung getragen. Das lang fließende Aodai mit dem hohen Stehkragen gab es schon im 17. Jahrhundert. Über die Jahrhunderte wurde es schlichter, das Oberteil enger und teilweise transparenter. Heute ist das Seidenhemd, das mit einer weiten Hose getragen wird, hauptsächlich Festgewand. Ideal für den Besuch eines Wasserpuppenspiels.

Mua Roi Nuoc – Wasserpuppentheater – gibt es nur in Vietnam. Das Delta des Roten Flusses sorgt in der Regenzeit für jährliches Hochwasser, auch heute noch, trotz des ausgeklügelten Netzes an Deichen. Die Bauern können während der Überschwemmung nicht aufs Feld; vermutlich aus Langeweile erdachten sie sich diese besondere

needs rice, just as a fish needs water.” 80 % of the rural population earn their living in this way. The rice paddies are found above all in the rice baskets of the river deltas. The landscape is dominated by the colour green in every imaginable shade. From the delicate nuances of young seedlings, to the rich and vivid green during growth and on to the yellow-green of harvest time. And in between, slowly-trudging water buffaloes with white egrets on their backs. Water buffaloes are the tractors of the rice-farmers, ploughing up the alluvial soil before the next harvest is sown. The peaceful cattle are usually ridden by children who pilot them through the fields.

The tapering conical hats of bast and the aodai, the long robe with the slits, round off the popular image of Vietnam. But these practical hats are now usually worn only by the rural population. The long, flowing aodai with the high vertical collar was worn as early as the 17th Century. Over the centuries it became simpler, the upper part more close-fitting and sometimes more transparent. Today the silk shirt, which is worn with white trousers, is generally worn for parties or celebrations. Ideal for a visit to the water puppet theatre.

Mua Roi Nuoc – water puppet theatre – is an entertainment unique to Vietnam. The delta of the Red River floods every year during the monsoon season, even today, despite the sophisticated network of dikes and embankments. The farmers cannot work the fields during the flooding, so it was probably out of boredom that they invented this special form of puppet theatre. As early as the 11th Century, farmers carved puppets out of fig wood, which served for

exemple ainsi qu'une constante surveillance aérienne ne leur sont d'aucune aide. Les Vietnamiens sortent certes vainqueurs de cette guerre contre les Américains – à l'instar de David gagnant contre Goliath – mais avant de quitter définitivement les lieux, les Américains auront largué plus de huit millions de tonnes de bombes, laissant derrière eux cinq millions de morts, dont 58 000 soldats américains. Ce pays à la population rurale est dévasté, les maisons détruites, la nature empoisonnée par le napalm et l'Agent Orange. Aujourd'hui encore, trois générations plus tard, il naît toujours des enfants souffrant de malformations. Le photographe de guerre américain, Philip Jones Griffith, a dit : « Les Français, eux au moins, ont laissé des cathédrales, des opéras et des gares. Les Américains par contre ont fait du Vietnam un véritable musée des horreurs. »

Ni un millénaire de domination chinoise, ni les colonisations successives française, japonaise et américaine, ni la partition de leur pays donnant naissance au Vietnam du Nord et au Vietnam du Sud, n'ont empêché les Vietnamiens de préserver leurs traditions ainsi que leurs habitudes culinaires. On trouve à la base de chaque repas le riz à partir duquel on fait des nouilles ou du papier avec lequel on confectionne ces rouleaux typiques. Le riz est la perle des Dieux. Un adage dit : «Tout être humain a besoin de riz pour vivre comme le poisson a besoin d'eau. » 80 % de la population globale gagne sa vie grâce au riz dont la culture est surtout pratiquée dans les paniers des deltas fluviaux. Dans ce paysage de rizières, les tons verts dominent : de la douce nuance des jeunes plants en passant par le vert vi-

un punto en el que ni las bombas de napalm, ni los desfoliantes, ni los herbicidas tóxicos como el "Agent Orange", ni la más exhaustiva vigilancia aérea podían cambiar su rumbo. Al final de la guerra los vietnamitas habían logrado efectivamente vencer a los americanos –David había vencido a Goliath– pero en el transcurso del conflicto éstos habían arrojado ocho millones de toneladas de bombas y provocado cinco millones de muertos entre los cuales también hay que lamentar los 58 000 soldados americanos caídos. Al final la tierra de los campesinos había quedado devastada, sus casas destruidas, la naturaleza envenenada con napalm y "Agent Orange". Aún hoy, tres generaciones más tarde, siguen naciendo niños con malformaciones. A este respecto el fotógrafo americano de guerra Philip Jones Griffith dijo: "Al menos los franceses dejaron catedrales, óperas y estaciones. Los americanos sin embargo han convertido Vietnam en un museo de los horrores".

Ni un milenio de dominio chino, ni las sucesivas colonizaciones francesa, japonesa y americana, ni la partición de su país en Vietnam del norte y del sur consiguieron arrebatarles a los vietnamitas sus tradiciones. Tampoco las gastronómicas. La base de cualquier comida es el arroz. Con él se fabrica pasta y hasta el papel con el que luego se elaboran los típicos rollitos. El arroz es la perla de los dioses. Un refrán vietnamita dice: "los hombres necesitan el arroz como los peces el agua". El 80 por ciento de la población rural se gana su sustento con el cultivo del arroz, que está especialmente extendido en los deltas de los ríos. En este paisaje predominan todos los tonos del verde: desde la suave tonalidad de los brotes tempranos pasando por el

o carta di riso, che viene lavorata in modo da formare i tipici involtini. Il riso è la perla degli dei. Un proverbio dice: "Ogni essere umano ha bisogno del riso come il pesce ha bisogno dell'acqua." L'80 percento della popolazione contadina guadagna il suo sostentamento coltivando riso. Le risaie si trovano soprattutto nei cosiddetti "cesti di riso" rappresentati dai delta dei due fiumi. Il colore verde determina in tutte le sue tonalità intermedie l'aspetto del paesaggio. Dalle delicate sfumature dei giovani avannotti al verde vivo e forte durante la crescita fino al giallo-verde al momento del raccolto. Tra i campi i bufali indiano che si muovono con passo pesante, sulla schiena bianchi aironi. I bufali indiani sono i trattori dei coltivatori di riso che arano i campi prima della semina. Perlopiù sono bambini che, seduti sui pacifici bovini, guidano questi ultimi attraverso i campi.

Gli appuntiti cappelli in rafia e l'AoDai, la lunga veste con i tagli, completano l'immagine del Vietnam dettata dal cliché. Ma i pratici copricapo vengono per la maggior parte indossati solo più dalla popolazione contadina. Il lungo e morbido AoDai con il colletto alto e rigido esisteva già nel XVII secolo. Lungo i secoli è divenuto sempre più semplice, la parte superiore si è ristretta ed è diventata in parte trasparente. Oggi la camicia di seta, che viene indossata con un ampio pantalone, è soprattutto un capo da festa. Ideale per assistere ad uno spettacolo di marionette null'acqua.

Mua Roi Nuoc – il teatro delle marionette acquatiche – esiste solo in Vietnam. Nella stagione delle piogge il delta del Fiume Rosso provoca ogni anno inondazioni, anche oggi, nonostante la sofisticata rete di argini. Durante tali periodi i contadini non possono andare nei campi, quindi, pro-

Form des Puppentheaters. Schon im elften Jahrhundert schnitzen Bauern Puppen aus Feigenholz, die beim Dorffest zur Unterhaltung dienen. Hinter einem Bambusvorhang verborgen, setzen die Künstler mit oft meterlangen Stangen, Stäben und Zugfäden Puppen in Bewegung. Feuerspuckend, in Rauch gehüllt rast ein Drache durch das Wasser, stolz erhobenen Hauptes steht König Le Loi in der Bootsmitte auf gefärbtem Wasser, eine perfekte Illusion. Die Puppenspieler stehen bis zum Bauch im Wasser. Wasser liefert nicht nur das Thema der Stücke, sondern ist auch selbst Medium.

Klares Wasser, schroffe Kalkkuppen und steil aufragende, überwucherte Felstürme bilden die einmalige Landschaft der Halong-Bucht. Sie hat etwas Unwirkliches, Tropisches und Traumhaftes, auch wegen des zarten Dunstes, der die bizarren Felsformationen oft nur schemenhaft erkennen lässt. 1994 hat die Unesco dieses Naturschauspiel zum Weltkulturerbe erklärt. Als Vietnam wieder einmal bedroht wurde, besagt die Legende, kam den Menschen eine Drachenmutter samt ihrer Kinder aus den Bergen zu Hilfe. Halong heißt absteigender Drache. Der spuckte 3000 Perlen ins Wasser, die zu zerklüfteten Felsinseln wuchsen. Den Angreifern war dadurch der Weg versperrt.

Perlen gab es auch in Hue, der Kaiserstadt, im Überfluss. Kaiser Tu Duc war der vierte von 13 vietnamesischen Herrschern. Er regierte von 1847 bis 1883 in Hue, der ehemaligen Hauptstadt. Die purpurne Stadt am Parfümfluss. Dort liegen die einst opulenten Grabanlagen der Herrscher, die zeitlebens ihren Vorlieben frönten. So hatte Tu Duc nicht nur 103 Konkubinen, sein Teewasser musste

entertainment at the village festival. Concealed behind a bamboo curtain, the artists control the movements of the puppets with rods and strings sometimes several feet long. Cloaked in smoke and fire, a dragon races through the water, while King Le Loi stands with head proudly raised in the middle of the boat on the coloured water, a perfect illusion. The puppet-masters stand up to their stomach in the water, which is not only the subject of the performances, but also the medium itself.

Clear water, jagged limestone knolls and steeply rising, overgrown rocky towers form the unique landscape of the Halong Bay. The place has something unreal, tropical and dreamlike about it, not least because of the delicate mist which sometimes reveals only the outlines of the bizarre rock formations. In 1994, UNESCO declared this natural play of nature to be a World Cultural Heritage site. When Vietnam was threatened once more, says legend, a female dragon and her children came out of the mountains to aid the people. Halong means "descending dragon". She spat 3,000 pearls into the water, which grew into jagged rocky islands, blocking the path of the invaders.

Pearls were also available in abundance in Hue, the city of the Emperor. Emperor Tu Duc was the fourth of 13 Vietnamese rulers. He reigned from 1847 to 1883 in Hue, the former capital. The purple city on the Perfume River. Here lie the once opulent tombs of the rulers, who always indulged their every whim. Tu Duc not only had 103 concubines, his tea water had to be collected from the dewdrops of the lotus blossom. His reign was splendid, although wasteful and expensive.

goureux de la phase de croissance jusqu'au vert jaunâtre de la récolte. Ce tableau ne saurait être complet sans les buffles qui pataugent lourdement dans les champs avec des hérons blancs juchés sur leur dos. Les riziculteurs les utilisent ici comme tracteurs pour labourer les terres alluvionnaires avant les semailles. La plupart du temps, ces bœufs pacifiques sont chevauchés par des enfants qui les guident à travers les champs.

Les chapeaux pointus en raffia et l'« aodai », longue tunique fendue complètent le cliché que l'on a du Vietnam. Pourtant, ces chapeaux pratiques ne sont en général portés que par la population rurale. La longue aodai avec son col remonté existait déjà au 17ème siècle, mais au cours du temps, cette tenue s'est simplifiée, le haut est devenu plus étroit et parfois plus transparent. Aujourd'hui, la chemise de soie portée avec un pantalon large est surtout un habit de fête.

De l'eau limpide, des cimes calcaires escarpées et des colonnes rocheuses abruptes couvertes de végétation forment le paysage singulier de la baie d'Halong. Ce décor un peu tropical semble entouré d'une aura irréelle et onirique ... Peut-être à cause de cette fine brume fantasmagorique qui laisse à peine entrevoir le contour de ces formations rocheuses bizarroïdes. En 1994, l'Unesco a inscrit ce paysage à son patrimoine culturel. Alors que le Vietnam est, une fois de plus, menacé, une légende raconte qu'une mère dragon aurait quitté avec ses petits les montagnes pour venir en aide à la population. Halong signifie « le lieu où le dragon descend ». Elle crache alors dans l'eau 3 000 perles qui se transforment en îlots rocheux déchiquetés, empêchant ainsi les assaillants d'aller plus loin.

vigoroso verde de la fase de crecimiento de la planta hasta el verdeamarillo del tiempo de la cosecha. Y en esta escena no podían faltar los pintorescos búfalos acuáticos de cansino paso con garzas blancas posadas sobre su lomo. Los búfalos acuáticos son los tractores de los campesinos del arroz. Con ellos aran los bancales de arroz antes de inundarlos para la siembra. A menudo son niños los que cabalgan y guían por los campos a estas pacíficas bestias.

Para redondear la imagen tópica de Vietnam solo quedan los típicos sombreros cónicos de rafia y el "aodai", la larga vestimenta con entalladuras. La verdad es que esos prácticos sombreros sólo se utilizan en el campo. En cuanto al "aodai", esta larga prenda de cuello alto ya existía en el siglo XVII. Con el tiempo fue haciéndose más simple en su conjunto. Su parte superior también se hizo más estrecha y a veces transparente. Hoy se lleva sobre todo en las fiestas en combinación con un amplio pantalón y normalmente está confeccionada de seda.

El singular paisaje de la bahía de Halong está constituido por aguas transparentes, escarpadas cimas calcáreas y abruptas columnas rocosas cubiertas de vegetación. Todo este escenario tropical aparenta estar envuelto de un aura irreal y onírica... Quizás se deba a la tenue y fantasmagórica neblina que apenas deja entrever el contorno de las formaciones rocosas de la bahía. En 1994 la Unesco declaró Patrimonio de la Humanidad este espectáculo natural. Una leyenda nos cuenta que en una ocasión en que Vietnam volvía a estar amenazado, una dragona acudió con sus hijos desde las montañas a ayudar a los hombres. Halong significa "dragón rampante". La dragona expulsó 3000

babilmente a causa della noia a ciò conseguente, essi hanno inventato questa particolare forma del teatro delle marionette. Già nell'undicesimo secolo i contadini intagliavano bambole in legno di fico che servivano all'intrattenimento nelle feste dei paesi. Nascosti dietro ad una tenda di bambù gli artisti, spesso con aste lunghe metri, bastoni e fili, mettevano in movimento le marionette. Un drago avvolto nel fumo sfreccia attraverso l'acqua sputando fuoco, il re Le Loi sta orgogliosamente in piedi a testa alta nella barca sull'acqua colorata, una perfetta illusione. I marionettisti sono immersi nell'acqua fino al ventre. L'acqua non costituisce solo l'argomento delle storie rappresentate, bensì è essa stessa il mezzo.

Acqua limpida, aspre punte di calcare e ripidi ed aguzzi scogli ricoperti di vegetazione costituiscono il singolare paesaggio della baia di Halong. Un ambiente che ha qualcosa di irreale, di tropico, da sogno, anche a causa del delicato vapore che spesso permette di individuare solo la sagoma dei bizzarri gruppi rocciosi. Nel 1994 l'Unesco ha dichiarato questo spettacolo naturale patrimonio culturale dell'umanità. La leggenda racconta che quando il Vietnam venne nuovamente minacciato, i suoi abitanti furono aiutati da una madre drago accorsa con i suoi figli dalle montagne. "Halong" significa "drago che scende". Esso sputò 3000 perle nell'acqua e queste divennero isole di rocce interrotte da gole che bloccarono il passaggio agli assalitori.

Di perle ve ne era in eccesso anche a Hue, la città dell'imperatore. L'imperatore Tu Duc era il quarto di tredici dominatori vietnamiti. Egli governò dal 1847 al 1883 a Hue, l'excapitale. La città purpurea in riva al Fiume dei Profumi. Qui

auch aus den Tautropfen der Lotusblume gesammelt werden. Prunkvoll, verschwenderisch und teuer war seine Herrschaft.
Ein Hauch von Prunk oder besser Kitsch liegt auch über dem Großen Tempel von Tay Ninh. Ein gelbes Dach mit rosa Pferdchen, rote Fensterläden, blaugelbe Balkone. Im Innenraum stehen mächtige Pfeiler von Drachen umschlungen. Der Tempel der Cao-Dai-Religion, die 1926 der Beamte Ngo Minh Chieu erfand. Er behauptete, ein Engel sei zu ihm gekommen mit dem himmlischen Auftrag, eine neue Religion zu gründen. Es entstand ein Gemenge aus Katholizismus, Konfuzianismus und Buddhismus. Päpste gibt es, Bischöfe, Priester und als Heilige fungieren etwa Shakespeare, Platon, Lenin, Jeanne d'Arc oder Victor Hugo. Von vier Millionen Gläubigen sprechen die Cao-Dai-Anhänger. Ihr bunter Tempel ist längst ein Touristenmagnet geworden. Tourismus ist in Vietnam eine Wachstumsbranche. Die meisten Besucher kommen aus China, den USA, Japan und Frankreich. Anfangs waren die Fremden hauptsächlich von Kriegsmuseen und dem kilometerlangen, unterirdischen Tunnelsystem der Widerstandskämpfer fasziniert. Mittlerweile stehen auch die Tempel und Pagoden, die Kolonialbauten, die quirligen Städte, die Bergwelt und vor allem die palmenbewachsenen, samtweichen Sandstrände mit grandiosen Tauchrevieren hoch im Kurs. Denn die Bambusstange mit den Reiskörben hat viel zu bieten.

A breath of splendour, or rather kitsch, also lies over the Great Temple of Tay Ninh. A yellow roof decorated with pink horses, red shutters and a blue and yellow balcony. In the interior stand massive pillars surrounded by dragons. The temple of the Cao-Dai religion, which was established in 1926 by the official Ngo Minh Chieu. He claimed that he had been visited by an angel, who gave him the divine command to found a new religion. This resulted in a mixture of Catholicism, Confucianism and Buddhism. There are popes, bishops, priests, and the panoply of the Saints is made up of such figures as Shakespeare, Plato, Lenin, Joan of Arc and Victor Hugo. Cao-Dai followers speak of four million adherents. Their gaudy temple has long since become a tourist magnet. Tourism is a growth industry in Vietnam. Most visitors come from China, the USA, Japan and France. At first, foreigners were mainly fascinated by the war museums and the miles of underground tunnel systems used by the resistance fighters. These have now been largely supplanted by the temples and pagodas, the colonial buildings, the bustling towns, the mountains and above all the palm-fringed, velvety-soft sand beaches with their luxurious diving facilities. Because the bamboo pole with its two rice baskets has much to offer.

Une aura d'ostentation pour ne pas dire de kitsch entoure le grand temple de Tay Ninh : un toit jaune avec de petits chevaux roses, des volets rouges, des balcons jaunes et bleus avec, à l'intérieur, des dragons enlaçant d'imposants piliers. C'est le temple de la religion caodaïste créée en 1926 par le fonctionnaire Ngo Minh Chieu. Il a affirmé qu'un ange lui serait apparu et lui aurait donné pour mission divine de fonder une nouvelle religion. Le résultat est un mélange de rites catholiques, confucianistes et bouddhistes avec des papes, des évêques et des saints parmi lesquels on retrouve par exemple Shakespeare, Platon, Lénine, Jeanne d'Arc ou Victor Hugo. Les adeptes du Caodaïsme parlent de quatre millions de croyants. Leur temple multicolore est depuis longtemps un pôle d'attraction pour les touristes. Le tourisme est d'ailleurs une branche en pleine expansion dans ce pays. La plupart des visiteurs viennent de Chine, des Etats-Unis, du Japon et de France. Au début, les touristes étaient surtout fascinés par les musées de la guerre et les nombreux tunnels souterrains de plusieurs kilomètres de long construits par la résistance pendant la guerre. Aujourd'hui, ils viennent également pour voir les temples et les pagodes, les édifices coloniaux, le dynamisme des villes, les montagnes et surtout les plages de sable doux plantées de palmiers avec d'incomparables sites de plongée. Le balancier en bambou avec ces paniers de riz n'a pas fini en effet de dévoiler toutes ses richesses.

perlas en el agua que se convirtieron en las escabrosas islas de la bahía. De esta manera los atacantes encontraron bloqueada su trayectoria.

El gran templo de Tay Ninh tiene un aura de ostentación, por no decir de cursilería: un tejado amarillo provisto de caballitos rosa, contraventanas rojas y balcones azules y amarillos. En su interior se erigen poderosos pilares rodeados de dragones. Se trata de un templo de la religión Cao-Dai, que fue inventada en 1926 por el funcionario Ngo Minh Chieu. Según sus declaraciones, un ángel se le apareció con un mandato divino: que estableciera una nueva religión. De esta forma surgió una mezcla de catolicismo, confucianismo y budismo. Hay papas, obispos y sacerdotes. Incluso santos. Entre ellos se cuentan Shakespeare, Platón, Lenin, Juana de Arco o Victor Hugo. Los propios fieles de Cao-Dai hablan de cuatro millones de creyentes. Hace ya tiempo que sus coloridos templos se convirtieron en una atracción turística. Lo que no es de extrañar, pues el turismo es uno de los nuevos sectores de fuerte crecimiento de Vietnam. La mayoría de los visitantes proviene de China, de los EE.UU., de Japón y de Francia. Al principio los turistas venían ante todo fascinados por los museos de guerra y por el sistema subterráneo de muchos kilómetros de túneles que la resistencia construyó durante la guerra. Pero las corrientes de viajeros ya han descubierto el resto de los encantos del país: los templos y las pagodas, la arquitectura colonial, el dinamismo de las ciudades, los paisajes de montaña y, sobre todo, las maravillosas playas y sus incomparables zonas de buceo. Y es que la caña de bambú con sus dos cestos de arroz tiene muchísimo que ofrecer.

si trovano le tombe una volta opulenti dei dominatori che quando erano in vita amavano abbandonarsi ai loro vizi. Tu Duc ad esempio non solo aveva 103 concubine, egli pretendeva anche che l'acqua con cui veniva preparato il suo tè fosse raccolta dalle gocce di rugiada del fiore di loto. Fasto, spreco e dispendio erano i connotati del suo dominio.

Un tocco di fasto o meglio di kitsch si riscontra anche sul Grande Tempio di Tay Ninh. Un tetto giallo con cavallini rosa, davanzali rossi, balconi giallo-blu. All'interno vi sono massicci pilastri avvolti da draghi. Il tempio della religione Cao Dai, inventata nel 1926 dall'impiegato statale Ngo Minh Chieu. Egli sosteneva che un angelo fosse venuto da lui per conferirgli la divina missione di fondare una nuova religione. Ne nacque un misto di cattolicesimo, confucianesimo e buddismo. Ci sono papi, vescovi, preti, e come santi troviamo ad esempio Shakespeare, Platone, Lenin, Giovanna d'Arco e Victor Hugo. I seguaci Caodaismo parlano di quattro milioni di credenti. Il loro variopinto tempio è diventato da lungo un'attrazione turistica. Il turismo in Vietnam è un settore in continua crescita. La maggior parte dei visitatori provengono dalla Cina, dagli USA, dal Giappone e dalla Francia. All'inizio gli stranieri erano affascinati principalmente dai musei di guerra e dal sistema di tunnel sotterranei costruito dagli eroi della resistenza lungo diversi chilometri. Adesso i turisti vengono attratti invece anche dai tempi e dalle pagode, dalle costruzioni coloniali, dalle vivaci città, dal mondo montano e soprattutto dalle spiagge di sabbia vellutata ricche di palme con meravigliose zone per fare immersione. Infatti il paese che sembra una canna di bambù con due cesti di riso ha molto da offrire.

1	Reunification Palace, Ho Chi Minh City
2	General Post Office, Ho Chi Minh City
3	Notre Dame Cathedral, Ho Chi Minh City
4	Ho Chi Minh City
5	Near My Tho, Mekong
6	Can Tho, Mekong
7	Vinh Long, Mekong
8	Can Tho, Mekong
9	Vinh Long, Mekong
10	Sand Dunes, Mui Ne
11 | 12	Mui Ne
13 | 14	Hoi An
15	Train station, Phan Rang
16	Hoi An
17	Japanese Bridge, Hoi An
18	Market, Hoi An
19	Da Nang
20	Nha Trang
21 | 22	Temple, My Son
23	Hai Van Pass (Pass of the Ocean Clouds)
24	Reunification Express, Hai Van Pass (Pass of the Ocean Clouds)
25	Imperial City, Hué
26 | 27 | 28 | 29	Forbidden Purple City, Citadel, Hué
30	Hué
31 | 32	Ba Be Lake
33	Cao Bang
34	Sapa
35 | 36	Ban Gioc Falls
37	Trung Khanh
38	Dong Dang
39 | 40	Ninh Binh
41	Cao Bang
42 | 43	Halong Bay
44	Floating village, Halong Bay
45	Ho Chi Minh Mausoleum, Hanoi
46 | 47	Temple of Literature, Hanoi
48	Hanoi
49	Turtle Temple, Hoan Kiem Lake, Hanoi
50	The Huc Bridge, Hoan Kiem Lake, Hanoi

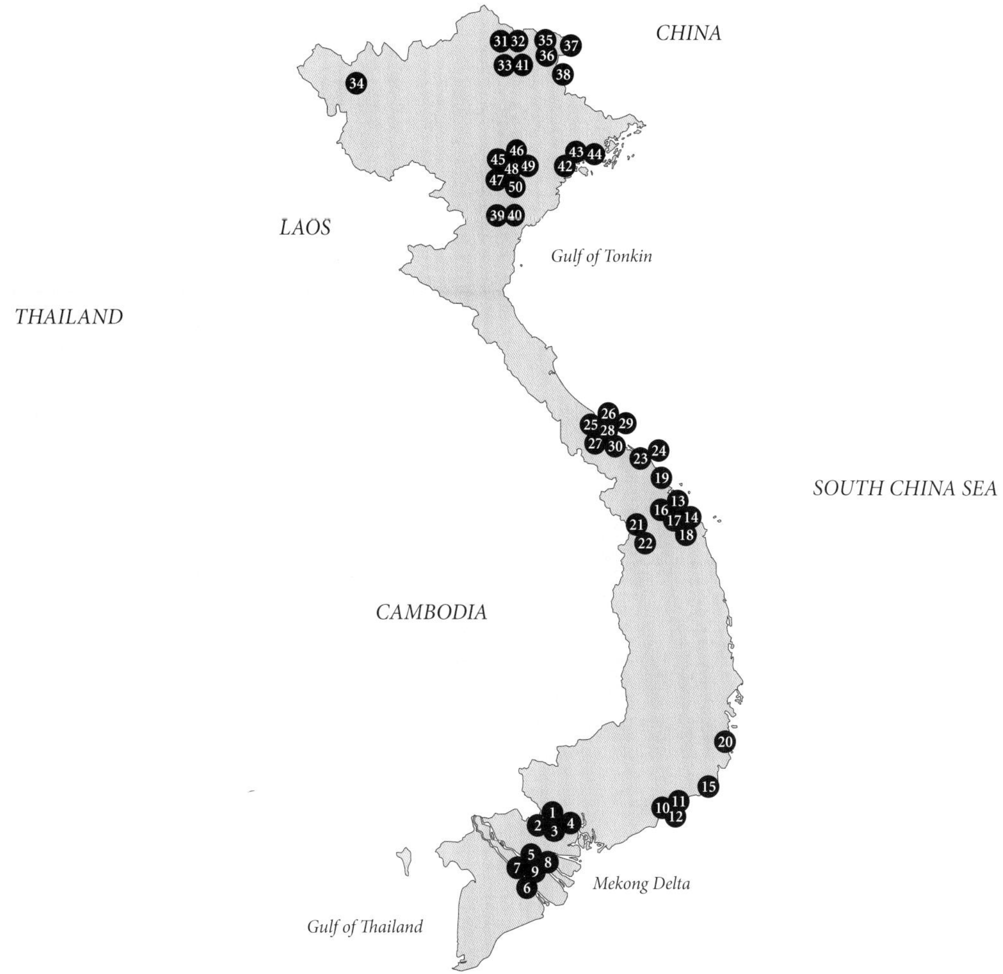
CHINA
LAOS
Gulf of Tonkin
THAILAND
SOUTH CHINA SEA
CAMBODIA
Mekong Delta
Gulf of Thailand
1
2
3
4
5
6
7
8
9
10
11
12
13
14
15
16
17
18
19
20
21
22
23
24
25
26
27
28
29
30
31
32
33
34
35
36
37
38
39
40
41
42
43
44
45
46
47
48
49
50

1 Reunification Palace, Ho Chi Minh City

2 General Post Office, Ho Chi Minh City

3 Notre Dame Cathedral, Ho Chi Minh City

DIAMOND PLAZA

5 Near My Tho, Mekong

► **6** Can Tho, Mekong

7 Vinh Long, Mekong

ĐIỆN GIA DỤNG
THUẦN
LINH THIỆT

 Can Tho, Mekong

► 9 Vinh Long, Mekong

10 Sand Dunes, Mui Ne

11 Mui Ne

13 Hoi An

▸ **15** Train station, Phan Rang

TOA

江山開聖開基千載

17 Japanese Bridge, Hoi An

► **18** Market, Hoi An

AIA
SPORT

19 Da Nang

► **21** Temple, My Son

22 Temple, My Son

23 Hai Van Pass (Pass of the Ocean Clouds)

24 Reunification Express, Hai Van Pass (Pass of the Ocean Clouds)

▸ 25 Imperial City, Hué

26 Forbidden Purple City, Citadel, Hué

27 Forbidden Purple City, Citadel, Hué

► **28** Forbidden Purple City, Citadel, Hué

29 Forbidden Purple City, Citadel, Hué

31 Ba Be Lake

► 32 Ba Be Lake

► **34** Sapa

35 Ban Gioc Falls

37 Trung Khanh

► **38** Dong Dang

39 Ninh Binh

41 Cao Bang

► **42** Halong Bay

43 Halong Bay

44 Floating village, Halong Bay

45 Ho Chi Minh Mausolcum, Hanoi

46 Temple of Literature, Hanoi

47 Temple of Literature, Hanoi

SINH CAFE
BOOKING
TIME

49 Turtle Temple, Hoan Kiem Lake, Hanoi

► **50** The Huc Bridge, Hoan Kiem Lake, Hanoi

ANITA DROBECK wurde 1975 in Heidelberg geboren. Nach dem Besuch einer Photographenschule absolvierte sie eine Ausbildung zur Photographin mit den Schwerpunkten People und Industrie. Es folgten mehrere freie Mitarbeiten bei verschiedenen Photographen, wo sie unter anderem Reportagen photographierte. 2001 machte sich Anita Drobeck als Photodesignerin selbstständig und eröffnete später mit ihrem Freund und Kollegen Nico Rademacher das Photostudio „studio visuell – photography" in Heidelberg.

NICO RADEMACHER wurde 1977 in Walldürn geboren. In den frühen 90er Jahren entdeckte er seine Leidenschaft für die Photographie. Nach mehreren freien Mitarbeiten bei verschiedenen Werbe- und Peoplephotographen und einer klassischen Photographenausbildung arbeitet er seit 2002 als freier Photodesigner. Gemeinsam mit Anita Drobeck betreibt Nico Rademacher seit 2004 das Photostudio „studio visuell – photography", mit den Schwerpunkten Werbe- und Peoplephotographie in Heidelberg.

IRIS LEMANCZYK wurde 1964 in Kirchheim/Teck bei Stuttgart geboren. Nach dem Studium der Germanistik und Geographie lockte immer wieder die Ferne. Sie reiste um die Welt, schnupperte eine Zeit lang Zirkusluft, lebte in Namibia und besuchte für ein paar Monate Australien und Neuseeland. Dazwischen arbeitete sie als Zeitungs-Redakteurin bei der „Südwest Presse" in Ulm. Seit 1997 ist sie freiberuflich tätig, schreibt Kinder- und Jugendbücher sowie Sachbücher, verfasst Reiseberichte und ist als Dozentin für Kreatives Schreiben tätig.

ANITA DROBECK was born in 1975 in Heidelberg. After attending a photographers' college, she completed her training as a photographer specialising in people and industry. This was followed by several periods of freelance work with various photographers, where she photographed news reports amongst other things. In 2001, Anita Drobeck went independent as a photographic designer, later opening the photo studio "studio visuell – photography" in Heidelberg with her friend and colleague Nico Rademacher.

NICO RADEMACHER was born in 1977 in Walldürn. In the early 1990s, he discovered his passion for photography. After several freelance jobs with various advertising and portrait photographers and classical photographer training, he has worked since 2002 as a freelance photographic designer. Together with Anita Drobeck, Since 2004 he runs the photo studio "studio visuell – photography" in Heidelberg, specialising in advertising and portrait photography.

IRIS LEMANCZYK was born in 1964 in Kirchheim/Teck near Stuttgart. After studying German and geography, she gave way to the call of far-distant places. She travelled around the world, experienced the circus life for a time, lived in Namibia and spent several months in Australia and New Zealand. In between, she also learnt something more conventional: newspaper editing with the "Südwest Presse" in Ulm. Since 1997 she has worked as a freelancer, writing children's books and non-fiction and compiling travel reports, and also works as a lecturer on creative writing.

ANITA DROBECK est née en 1975 à Heidelberg. Après des études dans une école de photographie, elle suit une formation de photographe pour se spécialiser dans les thèmes de la société et de l'industrie. Elle travaille ensuite en collaboration libre avec divers photographes. En 2001, Anita Drobeck s'installe à son compte en tant que photographe designer et ouvre plus tard l'atelier de photographie « studio visuell – photography » à Heidelberg.

NICO RADEMACHER est né en 1977 à Walldürn. Au début des années 90, il se découvre une passion pour la photographie. Après avoir suivi une formation classique professionnelle de photographe et travaillé en collaboration libre avec divers photographes spécialisés dans la publicité et les thèmes de société, il est, depuis 2002, photographe designer indépendant Avec Anita Drobeck, il dirige depuis 2004 l'atelier de photographie « studio visuell – photography ».

IRIS LEMANCZYK est née en 1964 à Kirchheim/Teck près de Stuttgart. Après des études de philologie allemande et de géographie, elle effectue régulièrement des voyages lointains. Elle voyage à travers le monde, séjourne pendant quelque temps dans un cirque, vit en Namibie et passe plusieurs mois en Australie et en Nouvelle-Zélande. Entre toutes ces occupations, elle travaille comme rédactrice journalistique au quotidien allemand « Südwest Presse » à Ulm. Depuis 1997, elle travaille comme rédactrice indépendante, écrit des livres destinés à l'enfance et à la jeunesse ainsi que des livres d'essai. Elle rédige également des comptes rendus de voyage et dispense des cours de création littéraire.

ANITA DROBECK nació en 1975 en Heidelberg. Tras terminar sus estudios en una escuela de fotografía, realizó una ampliación de estudios para especializarse en la fotografía de temas de sociedad e industria. A continuación trabajó con diferentes fotógrafos en varias colaboraciones libres. En 2001 Anita Drobeck inició su carrera como diseñadora independiente de fotografía y poco más tarde inauguró en Heidelberg el estudio de fotografía "studio visuell – photography".

NICO RADEMACHER nació en 1977 en Walldürn. Descubrió su pasión por la fotografía a principios de los años 90. Tras concluir una clásica formación profesional como fotógrafo y realizar varias colaboraciones libres con fotógrafos especializados en publicidad y en temas de sociedad , en 2002 empezó a trabajar como diseñador libre de fotografía. Desde 2004 Nico Rademacher regenta con su colega Anita Drobeck el estudio de fotografía „studio visuell – photography".

IRIS LEMANCZYK nació en 1964 en el pueblo de Kirchheim/ Teck (Alemania). Tras terminar su carrera de Filología Germánica y Geografía se dejó atraer cada vez más por el encanto de los destinos exóticos: viajó por el mundo, experimentó durante algún tiempo la vida en un circo, residió en Namibia y pasó algunos meses en Australia y Nueva Zelanda. Y entre todas esas ocupaciones todavía encontró tiempo para aprender un oficio serio: redactora de periódicos en la editorial alemana "Südwest Presse" de Ulm. Desde 1997 trabaja como redactora libre y escribe diversos libros: desde literatura infantil y juvenil a libros de texto. Además confecciona relatos de viaje e imparte seminarios de creación literaria.

ANITA DROBECK è nata nel 1975 ad Heidelberg. Dopo aver frequentato una scuola di fotografia concluse un corso di fotografia specializzandosi sul tema delle persone e dell'industria. Seguirono varie libere collaborazioni con diversi fotografi presso i quali realizzò inoltre fotografie di reportage. Nel 2001 Anita Drohbeck iniziò un'attività in proprio come fotodesigner ed in seguito aprì insieme al compagno e collega Nico Rademacher lo studio fotografico „studio visuell – photography" in Heidelberg.

NICO RADEMACHER è nato nel 1977 a Walldürn. Nei primi anni novanta scoprì la sua passione per la fotografia. Dopo numerose collaborazioni libere con vari fotografi di persone e nella pubblicità ed una formazione classica in campo fotografico dal 2002 lavora come fotodesigner indipendente. Insieme ad Anita Drobeck dal 2004 Nico Rademacher esercita nello studio fotografico "studio visuell – photography" ad Heidelberg.

IRIS LEMANCZYK è nata nel 1964 a Kirchheim/Teck vicino a Stoccarda. Dopo la laurea in Lingua e Letteratura Tedesca e in Geografia ha seguito la sua passione per i viaggi in paesi lontani. È stata in tutto il mondo, per un certo periodo ha respirato l'aria del circo, ha vissuto in Namibia e per qualche mese ha abitato in Australia e Nuova Zelanda. Tra un viaggio e l'altro si è dedicata alla più razionale attività di redattrice presso la Südwest Presse di Ulm. Dal 1997 lavora come libera professionista, scrive libri per bambini e ragazzi e testi di saggistica, redige reportage di viaggi ed insegna scrittura creativa.

ISBN: 978-3-89823-352-1

Concept: Bernhard Wipfler, Sebastian Wipfler, Marcus Bela Schmitt
Design: Designgruppe Fanz & Neumayer | Marcus Bela Schmitt & EDITION PANORAMA | Diana May
Editorial Department: Dr. Michael Barchet, Wolfgang Roth
Translations: Global-Text Fachübersetzungen, Heidelberg | Mark Woolfe, Jocelyne Abarca, Dr. Maria Carasi, Sebastián González Mohíno
Separations: EPS GmbH, Speyer
Printing: ColorDruck Leimen GmbH
Bookbinding: Buchbinderei Schaumann GmbH, Darmstadt

EDITION PANORAMA GmbH
G 7, 14
D - 68159 Mannheim
www.editionpanorama.com

A production by EDITION**PANORAMA**